Booker T. Washington

JUNIOR ▪ WORLD ▪ BIOGRAPHIES

A JUNIOR BLACK AMERICANS OF ACHIEVEMENT BOOK

Booker T. Washington

LOIS P. NICHOLSON

CHELSEA JUNIORS

a division of CHELSEA HOUSE PUBLISHERS

FRONTISPIECE: *Black leader and educator Booker T. Washington*

English-language words that are italicized in the text can be found in the glossary at the back of the book.

Chelsea House Publishers

EDITORIAL DIRECTOR   Richard Rennert
PRODUCTION MANAGER   Pamela Loos
ART DIRECTOR   Sara Davis
PICTURE EDITOR   Judy Hasday
SENIOR PRODUCTION EDITOR   Lisa Chippendale

Staff for BOOKER T. WASHINGTON

SENIOR EDITOR   John Ziff
ASSOCIATE EDITOR   Therese De Angelis
EDITORIAL ASSISTANT   Kristine Brennan
DESIGNER   Alison Burnside
PICTURE RESEARCHER   Sandy Jones
COVER ILLUSTRATION   Bill Donahey

3 5 7 9 8 6 4

Library of Congress Cataloging-in-Publication Data

Nicholson, Lois, 1949-
        Booker T. Washington / Lois P. Nicholson.
        p. cm.—(Junior Black Americans of achievement)
Includes bibliographical references and index.
Summary: Covers the life of Booker T. Washington from his early childhood as a Virginia slave through his rise to founder of the Tuskegee Institute.
        ISBN 0-7910-2388-5 (hc)
        ISBN 0-7910-4461-0 (pbk)
        1. Washington, Booker T., 1856-1915—Juvenile literature. 2. Afro-Americans—Biography—Juvenile literature. 3. Educators—United States—Biography—Juvenile literature. [1. Washington, Booker T., 1856-1915. 2. Educators. 3. Afro-Americans—Biography.]
I. Title. II. Series.
E185.97.W4N53 1997   96-52428
370'.92—dc21   CIP
[B]   AC

Contents

Plantation slaves react as a Union soldier reads the Emancipation Proclamation, which declared them free. When he was about eight years old, Booker had a similar experience as he stood on his master's front porch with the other slaves.

1

Freedom

The young slave boy lay upon the mound of rags piled on the dirt floor of his family's small log cabin. His sleep was disturbed by the voices of his mother and the other slaves. The April night was filled with their songs of praise and freedom lifting heavenward.

Booker, a light-skinned child, gazed at his older brother and younger sister sleeping nearby. He watched his mother, Jane, moving about the 14-by-16-foot room, singing while she worked.

She was the *plantation*'s cook, so not only was her small cabin home, but it also served as the kitchen for the entire plantation.

Booker, who was about eight years old, was like many slave children in that he did not know the exact date of his birth or the identity of his father. And while he often heard the other slaves singing, on this night it sounded different. Not only were the voices louder than usual, but they conveyed more joy than sorrow. The songs continued late into the night. They flowed through the windowless openings in the cabin's walls, as full and strong as the cold winds that chilled the slaves in winter.

Earlier that evening, someone from the "big house," where the master and his family lived, had come to the slaves' quarters and told them there would be a meeting at the big house the next morning. The slaves did not have to be told what the meeting was about.

For four years, the Civil War had raged around their Virginia home. The rest of their lives would be determined by its outcome: if the Union army of the North defeated the Confederate forces of the South, the slaves would be freed. If the South won, Booker and the others would remain the property of their owners, with no hope for a better life.

In recent months, the slaves had heard news of great victories by the Union army. They had watched a steady stream of Confederate soldiers, wearing ragged clothes and nursing severe wounds, make their way home through the surrounding forests. It seemed to the slaves the war would soon be over.

In the morning, the slaves were summoned to the front porch of the big house. Among them were white-haired old men and women, some 70 or 80 years old, who had lived their entire lives as slaves. The master's family waited on the porch. They watched grimly as a stranger, who seemed to be a government official, stood up and read at length from a paper he held before him. When he finished, he looked up

It was with mixed emotions that Booker and his family prepared to leave the plantation of James and Elizabeth Burroughs (pictured here). Washington would later recall that Mr. and Mrs. Burroughs, their 14 children, and their 10 slaves lived "very much like members of one big family."

and told the slaves they were now free people. They could go whenever and wherever they wished.

With tears of happiness streaming down her cheeks, Booker's mother bent down and

kissed her children, explaining to them what had just happened. The air rang with cries of jubilation and thanksgiving; the slaves were free at last. They expressed no hatred or bitterness toward their former masters, who sat silently on the porch. There had been little cruelty or mistreatment on this plantation. But underneath the joy of this occasion was some sadness at the breaking up of what was, for many, the only family they had ever known.

The celebration was short-lived, for when the slaves returned to their cabins, they faced a frightening new reality. They were free to go, but where? And how? They had no money, no possessions, no jobs, no other places to go. They could not read or write. Some of them had limited skills—like Jane, whose specialty was cooking—but none of them knew anything of the world beyond the plantation.

But freedom was too sweet not to be tasted. Every slave who could walk ventured off the property, at least for a few days or weeks, just to see what it felt like to be free. Then many—especially the older ones—returned "home" and arranged to continue working for their masters as free laborers.

Booker was lucky. About five years

earlier, his mother had married Washington Ferguson, a slave from a nearby plantation, in a secret slave wedding ceremony. Ferguson had escaped his master in 1864 and made his way over the Blue Ridge Mountains to the free state of West Virginia. He had worked and saved and bought his own home. Now, with the war over and the slaves freed, he sent a wagon to bring Jane and her children to live with him. Rescued from a life of slavery, Booker took his first steps on a journey that would lead him to become the first great leader of the African-American people.

This cabin in Hale's Ford, Virginia, is Booker T. Washington's birthplace. The cabin and the big house on the Burroughs plantation have been restored and turned into a national monument to honor Washington and his achievements.

2

Born into Slavery

When Booker was born near the tiny village of Hale's Ford in southwestern Virginia, his mother, Jane, was a slave. She could not read or write, and the births and deaths of slaves often went unrecorded. So Booker never knew exactly when his birthday was, but the best estimate is April 5, 1856. Nor did he know his father, who was probably a white man: Booker had light tan skin, reddish hair, and gray eyes.

The log cabin in which he was born

belonged to a farmer named James Burroughs, who owned about 10 slaves, including his mother, his sister Amanda, his brother John, and Booker himself. When Booker was old enough to work, he was described not by his age, but by his value on the slave market: $400.

Although the slaves on the Burroughs farm worked hard from sunup to sundown and lived in poverty and despair, their master—unlike many slave owners—was not a cruel man. In fact, he and his sons usually worked alongside their slaves in the fields of tobacco, wheat, corn, oats, flax, and sweet potatoes that supported his large family of 14 children. Despite the differences in their living conditions, they were, as Booker later recalled, "very much like members of one big family."

Since Jane's cabin was the plantation's kitchen, its open fireplace provided welcome heat in winter, but made the cabin stifling in the summer. The best food was carried to the big house for the Burroughs family. Jane had little time for her children, who never sat down to a meal together. It they were lucky, they scooped leftovers out of a pot or a skillet. They ate scraps of bread or drank milk whenever they found it. One of Booker's earliest memories was of his mother magically producing a chicken (actually stolen from the barnyard) late one night and cooking it for them.

Sweet potatoes were stored in a deep pit covered by a board in the middle of the cabin. Sometimes Booker treated himself to one or two, roasting them on the coals of the fireplace. Once, he watched hungrily while a party of young ladies from the big house ate ginger cakes in the yard. His mouth watered and he would have given anything he owned—if he had owned anything—to taste such a delicacy.

Wartime shortages of such *staples* as coffee, tea, and sugar affected the masters more than the slaves, whose basic diet of pork scraps and cornbread came from the farm. Their dreary diet remained much the same during the war.

When Booker was old enough to walk, he was put to work. Playtime was limited to occasional games of marbles or hide-and-seek with his siblings. Booker cleaned the yards, filled the potato hole, hauled water to the field workers, and carried books for the young Burroughs girls when they walked to school. He would peer enviously into the one-room schoolhouse, where white boys and girls sat looking over their books, because he longed to learn and study, too.

The job Booker dreaded most was taking corn to the mill for grinding. The mill was three miles away through dense forests. A heavy bag of corn was placed on a horse's back—along with Booker, who was still a little boy. On the way, the load usually shifted and fell off the horse, taking him down with it. He was too small to lift the sack, so he had to wait for someone to come along and help him. Sometimes hours went by, during which he could do little but sit and cry. When that happened, it would be dark before he returned from the mill. The Civil War was under way, and deserters from the Confederate army often hid in the woods. Booker had heard that deserters would cut off a Negro boy's ears if they found him alone in the forest. That prospect, and fear of the punishment he would get for being late, made him tremble on the days he had to go to the mill.

The only clothing Booker had was a long linen shirt woven from the coarsest part of the flax plant. It felt like a sandpaper shirt with hundreds of pins stuck in it. To spare Booker the scratches and welts a new shirt would make on his skin, his older brother, John, sometimes broke it in for him by wearing it for a few weeks. Booker's first shoes were made from an inch-thick piece of wood and a rough strap of leather.

Sometimes Booker was told to go to the big house to work the fly-chaser while the family ate. He pulled on a rope that operated a set of large paper fans hanging above the table to keep flies away. As he watched the Burroughs family eat, Booker listened to them talk about the war and the possibility of the slaves being freed by President Lincoln. One of the Burroughs boys, "Mars' Billy," had been killed in the fighting, and two others were wounded. These sorrows were felt almost as deeply among the slaves as they were in the big house. The slaves recalled Mars' Billy's kindness to them, and they tended to the wounded Burroughs boys with sincere devotion.

Booker would lie awake at night listening to the hushed conversations of the slaves. They relied on the spoken word to keep themselves abreast of what was happening in the world outside the plantation. Whoever was sent to the post office to get the mail, for instance, would listen to the whites talking about the war, then come back and report all he overheard. This was before radio or television, and the big-city newspapers were far away from Hale's Ford. Therefore, the "grapevine telegraph" was the

A 19th-century Virginia schoolhouse, probably much like the one the Burroughs girls attended. Booker, who carried the girls' books, longed to learn and study, too.

slaves' only source of information. It worked well, though: the slaves were often as well informed as their masters—and even got some news first.

Until he heard his mother praying for President Lincoln's armies to win the war and free her and her children, Booker was not aware that he was a slave, or of what slavery meant. He had never known any other way of life.

Although the slaves on the Burroughs plantation prayed for a Union victory, they wished no harm to their masters. Anticipating the appearance of Yankee soldiers, the family had buried their silver and other valuables in the forest. The slaves would gladly supply food and other aid to the soldiers of the Northern army, but they would never betray their masters by disclosing the location of the treasure. Remembering his devotion to the Burroughs family, Booker later wrote, "In order to defend and protect the women and children who were left on the plantations when the white males went to war, the slaves would have laid down their lives."

This kind of relationship between slaves and masters was not typical, but it was the reason that everyone felt like a family was being split up on that April morning when the Burroughs slaves were freed. And it was reflected in Booker's later pleas for friendly cooperation between blacks and whites in order to secure a better future for everyone.

When Booker and his family set out for Malden, West Virginia, in the wagon that Jane's husband, Washington Ferguson, had sent for them, they had no money—and no idea that their journey would take them more than 200 miles over rugged mountains. Because her health was poor, Jane rode most of the way in the wagon while the children walked. At night, they slept on the ground and cooked their food over an open fire. One night, they came upon an abandoned log cabin and decided to sleep under its roof. When Jane lit a fire in the fireplace, a long black snake dropped down from the chimney and slithered across the floor. They slept outside that night, too.

After several weeks they arrived in the

town of Malden. Booker's first taste of freedom was disappointing. The cabin his stepfather had readied for them was no better than the one they had left. It sat in a cluster of homes crowded close together, surrounded by filth and trash. Booker was used to breathing the fresh air of the countryside, not the foul smells of garbage and human waste. Drinking, gambling, and fighting went on all around them. In addition, Booker did not know his stepfather well. As a slave on another plantation, Washington Ferguson had only been able to visit his family about once a year before his escape.

The biggest industries in the area were salt and coal mining. Ferguson worked in a salt furnace, where salt was dried and shoveled into barrels. He immediately got Booker and John jobs at the furnace. To Booker, freedom now meant working harder than he ever had as a slave. He often began work at four o'clock in the morning. What little money the brothers earned was pocketed by their stepfather.

Soon after their arrival, a school for black children was opened in the neighboring town of Tinkersville, about a mile from Malden. Booker's desire to learn was relentless, but his stepfather made him continue working in the salt furnace. Watching other children pass by him on the way to and from school each day only made him more determined to find a way to join them.

A salt mine on the Kanawha River. After his family moved to Malden, a town in the Kanawha valley, Booker went to work packing salt with his stepfather and brother.

3

Seeds of Knowledge

Booker was now 10 or 11 years old and unable to read or write. The first written symbol he learned was the number 18, the number assigned to his stepfather at the salt furnace. At the end of the workday the boss would mark each barrel he and his stepsons had packed with "18." For a long time that was the only symbol Booker could identify.

One day his mother handed him an old spelling book. He never knew how she had obtained it, but it became his most treasured possession. Nobody in Booker's family could read, so he had to study the alphabet by himself. His mother encouraged him to learn, but she could not help him.

There was no public money to pay the teacher at the black school, so the parents of the students agreed to take turns feeding and boarding him in their homes. Although Booker was not a student at the school, his mother agreed to invite the teacher to join them for meals one day each month. Booker eagerly looked forward to the teacher's visits and was soon receiving private lessons at night.

After months of pleading with his stepfather, Booker finally won permission to go to school for a few months of the year. But he had to continue working at the same time. He worked from four o'clock in the morning until nine, and returned to work after school for a few more hours.

Booker faced three unexpected problems

in going to school. Classes began at nine, and he had to work until nine. The school was some distance from his job, so he always arrived late. He tried to trick his boss at work by moving the hands of the furnace clock a half hour ahead, so it read 9:00 when it was really only 8:30. The boss soon caught on.

His second problem was his *inadequate* clothing. All the other boys wore caps to school. His mother could not afford to buy him one, so she sewed two pieces of cloth together, and Booker had his cap. The other boys teased him about his crude homemade cap, but Booker wore it proudly.

Booker's third problem was that he didn't know his full name. The first time he heard his teacher call the attendance roll, he noticed that all the other boys answered to two or even three names. Booker had no middle or last name. Some slaves had adopted their masters' last names. When they were freed, many had dropped those names and chosen new ones.

Booker's family had done neither. When the teacher got to him, the first thing that came to Booker's mind was his father's first name, so he replied, "Booker Washington." Years later, he discovered that his mother had given him the name "Booker Taliaferro" (TOL-uh-ver). As a teenager he used Booker T. Washington as his full name.

Unable to maintain his grueling schedule, Booker soon had to drop out of school and work all day at the salt furnace. He tried to find someone to tutor him at night—without success, because Booker often knew more than his supposed teachers did. He was so determined to get an education that he sometimes walked over a mile each way to attend the night school in Tinkersville even though this left him with very little time for sleep. He was then put to work in a coal mine, where he had to walk a mile through dark underground tunnels to find a section where coal was being dug. Sometimes he got lost. If the flame in his lantern went out, he had to make his way through total blackness until he found someone to relight it. There was also the constant danger of the mine collapsing. For obvious reasons, Booker hated this job even more than working at the salt furnace.

One day, he heard about a job at the home of General Ruffner, who owned the coal mine and the salt furnace. His wife, Viola, had trouble keeping house servants because she was very strict. She demanded that every chore be done promptly and perfectly. Everything had to be kept neat and clean and in repair. But to Booker, it sounded better than working in a coal mine, and it paid five dollars a month. He landed the job, and eventually moved into the Ruffners' home.

His experience with Mrs. Ruffner made a permanent impression on Booker. For the rest of his life, he demanded neatness, cleanliness, and honesty from himself and others. He earned Mrs. Ruffner's trust, and she encouraged him to pursue his education. She gave him some books and allowed him to attend the school for an hour a day. At night, Booker hired teachers to work with him. Throughout his life, Booker often said, "The lessons I learned in the home of Mrs. Ruffner were as valuable to me as any education I have ever gotten anywhere else."

While he was working in the coal mine, Booker overheard some men talking about a school for black students called the Hampton Normal and Agricultural Institute. It was somewhere in Virginia; he did not know how far away from Malden it was. The men said that even poor students could go there if they worked to pay their expenses while they learned a trade. To Booker, it sounded like heaven. He vowed then and there to get to Hampton somehow, and never forgot this promise to himself during the year that he lived with the Ruffners.

When he was about 16, Booker decided it was time to set out for Hampton. But he had no money. Everything he had earned had gone to pay his family's household expenses. The former

Even before his stepfather allowed Booker to attend the black school in Tinkersville, his mother invited the teacher, William Davis (shown here), to eat meals with her family once a month. Booker savored these visits by Mr. Davis, who later became his first teacher.

slaves who lived in Malden prized education as much as Booker did. Many of the old, white-haired men and women went to the night school to learn to read: their dearest wish was to be able to read the Bible. When they heard that Booker wanted to go away to school to make a better life for himself, they collected hard-earned nickels and dimes, old pieces of clothing, and a little food for his journey. Booker said good-bye to his mother. She was in poor health, and he feared he would never see her again.

One morning in the fall of 1872 Booker set out for Hampton, which was 500 miles away. The train could take him only a short distance; the rest of the journey would have to be made by stagecoach. But Booker soon realized that his money would take him only part of the way. One night the stagecoach stopped at an old house that had been converted into a hotel. The other passengers, all of whom were white, took rooms for the night and sat down to supper. Before Booker could open his mouth to plead for a little food and a bed, the innkeeper ordered him out of the house.

"This was my first experience in finding out what the color of my skin meant," he recalled years after the incident.

The nights were cold in the mountains. Booker tried to stay warm by walking about all night. A few days later his money ran out. He walked and begged rides on wagons. In this way a tired, dirty, and hungry Booker reached the city of Richmond late one night. He still had 82 miles left on his journey.

Richmond was the first big city he had ever seen. He walked the streets, passing food stands piled high with fried chicken and apple pies. The sight and smell of good food made his empty stomach growl. Weak and exhausted, he came to a street with a boardwalk that was a few feet above street level. He crawled under the planks and slept while the boots of passersby thumped over his head.

In the morning he noticed that he was near the docks where ships were unloading their cargo. Booker got a few hours of work on the docks and worked there for several days after that. Working by day and sleeping under the boardwalk at night, he soon saved enough to pay his fare to Hampton.

When Booker finally stood before the three-story red brick building that was the Hampton school, he had 50 cents in his pocket. Hungry, dirty, and bedraggled, he looked more like a tramp than a student. He had completed his journey, but now he had to be admitted to the school. The head teacher, a stern woman from Vermont named Miss Mackie, looked him over and told him to stay in her waiting room. Booker watched while other students came through and gained admission. He believed that he could do as well as any of them, if only he got the chance.

After he had spent a few hours in anxious waiting, Miss Mackie said to him, "The adjoining recitation room needs sweeping. Take the broom and sweep it."

Booker eagerly took the broom and went to work. He was grateful that he had learned from Mrs. Ruffner how to remove every speck of dust from a room. He swept the floor three times and dusted everything four times. When he was satisfied, he reported to Miss Mackie, who inspected the room by wiping her handkerchief on the woodwork and on every table and bench. Booker watched, confident that the handkerchief would come up spotless.

Finally she said, "I guess you will do to enter this institution." She gave him a position as a janitor, which would pay for most of his living expenses.

Booker was elated to have passed this strange college entrance examination. For the first time in his life, he felt that he was where he belonged. To get there, Booker had emerged from slavery, endured poverty, worked in a salt furnace and a coal mine, and completed an *arduous* 500-mile journey. It all taught him a lesson he never forgot: "Success has to be measured not so much by the position that one has reached in life as by the obstacles which he has overcome while trying to succeed."

As a young man attending the Hampton Institute, Booker T. Washington learned to take pride in his appearance as well as his work. Good grooming became so important to him that Washington would later preach "the gospel of the toothbrush" to his own students.

4

A Quest to Learn

At the Hampton Institute, Booker had more to learn than what he could find in books. Until he was 10 years old, he had never even slept in a bed; at Hampton, he found one with two sheets on it. He did not know what to do with them, so he slept under both sheets the first night and on top of them the next. Then he finally noticed that the seven other students in his *dormitory* slept between their bedsheets. He had never eaten meals at scheduled times or sat at a table draped with a cloth. Napkins were new to him, too. And he had never seen a toothbrush or a bathtub. Of all Booker's new experiences, cleanliness and good grooming made the deepest impressions.

Booker had no money to pay the $70 annual tuition or to buy books. The only clothes he owned were on his back. Luckily, his willingness to work hard and his desire to learn were noticed and rewarded. The head of the school, General Armstrong, had arranged for a Massachusetts businessman, Mr. Morgan, to pay Booker's tuition. Northern charities sent barrels of used clothing for freed slaves, and much of Booker's wardrobe came from them. His brother John helped him with money occasionally, and he borrowed the books he could not afford to buy.

Most of the several hundred Hampton students were older than Booker. They were all former slaves, or freedmen. Almost all of them had to work to cover some of their costs. But they were determined to educate themselves to better support their families and to help their people prosper. The teachers were white Northerners. Booker was impressed by their interest in seeing the students succeed. He always called General Armstrong, who had been a leader of the Union army, the greatest man he ever knew.

At the end of his first year, Booker had no money to go home. He also owed the school $16 in board fees his work had not covered. That summer he worked in a restaurant. One day, he found a $10 bill under a table. He thought he should show it to the restaurant owner—even though he knew that $10 could have paid off most of his debt to Hampton. When Booker turned in the money, the owner kept it. Although he ended the summer still owing $16, he could be proud of his honesty—and the school let him pay back his debt a little bit at a time.

In addition to taking classes, Booker cared for the school's livestock, studied the Bible, and took lessons in public speaking. He became active in the school's debating society, where he discovered he had a talent for speaking *persuasively*.

After completing his second year, Booker found a way to return home for the summer. His mother and family and everyone else who had helped him get to school were happy to see him and to hear of his adventures at Hampton. But Booker could not find work in Malden: the salt furnace had closed, and the coal miners were out on strike. One night, while he was away from home searching for work, Jane died. He had not been able to fulfill his dream of providing a better life for his mother, but he was still determined to succeed in the world.

Without Jane, Booker's family life in Malden was difficult. His sister, Amanda, was too young to keep the house clean and prepare meals regularly. Booker found some work with his former employer, Mrs. Ruffner, and at a distant coal mine. These two jobs earned him enough to finance his trip back to Hampton to

Hampton's founder, General Samuel C. Armstrong. Washington considered him the greatest man he ever knew.

General Samuel C. Armstrong

begin his third year there in the fall.

The freed slaves' quest for better lives swelled the rosters at schools like Hampton. There was not enough room in the crowded dormitories. When General Armstrong put up tents on the grounds and asked the senior students to occupy them for the year, Booker volunteered. Despite the freezing winter winds, the students were happy to do whatever they could to help General Armstrong, the man they revered.

Booker graduated from Hampton in June of 1875, having earned the honor of speaking at the *commencement* exercises. In addition to his book learning, he had discovered that there was nothing undignified about hard manual labor—no matter how educated one became.

Booker still had no money when he graduated. He borrowed money to travel to a hotel in Connecticut, where he worked as a waiter for the summer. He saved enough to return to Malden, where he was hired as a teacher at the black school in nearby Tinkersville. The older freed slaves, as well as the children, wanted to learn how to read; Booker taught both a day and a night class. He also gave private lessons, started a reading group and debating society, and taught two Sunday school classes. He introduced his younger students to the comb, soap and water, and the toothbrush.

Despite his small income, Booker helped his older brother, John, attend Hampton. After he graduated, Booker and John both helped their brother James, who had been adopted by their mother, to study at Hampton also.

The years following the Civil War were called the Reconstruction—the readmission of the Confederate states into the Union. It was a time of turmoil and conflict. The freed slaves, who had no education or experience of the world beyond their plantations, were suddenly citizens with the legal right to vote. Some whites from the North, called *carpetbaggers*, came south for personal gain, cheating and taking advantage of the former slaves' inexperience as free people. Another group, called the Ku Klux Klan, was eager to deny black people their rights to jobs, votes, or property. While living in Malden, Booker saw white-hooded Klansmen terrify black people by burning their homes, schools, and churches—and by shooting or *lynching* anyone who opposed the Klan.

As disturbing as white hostility was, Booker was equally dismayed by the many blacks who presented themselves as teachers,

Hampton students drill on the campus lawn. The school's emphasis on self-discipline and hard work agreed with Washington's diligent nature, and he became a model student.

preachers, and politicians when they themselves could barely read. He became convinced that only through education, hard work, and training for well-paid professions could blacks make the *economic* progress that would earn them the respect and acceptance of their white neighbors. He believed that ignorant people—black or white—who did not contribute to their communities did not deserve to vote. Although he was offered chances to run for political office in West Virginia, he decided to devote his life to educating his race.

After teaching in Tinkersville for two years, during which he prepared many of his students to go on to Hampton, Booker traveled to Washington, D.C., to study at Wayland Seminary, a training school for Baptist ministers. There he was deeply disturbed to see many blacks who, in his opinion, spent their earnings foolishly, depended on the federal government too much, and considered a little education a license to avoid working hard. He also felt that Wayland's *curriculum* focused too much on *liberal arts* like Greek and Latin and not enough on "life and its conditions." He dropped out after only half a year.

In the summer of 1879, Booker received an invitation to teach at Hampton. Unlike his first journey to the institute, during which he had to walk much of the way, this time he could afford to ride the train the entire way. The school had invited the Kiowa and Cheyenne Indians to send their young people east to be educated at Hampton. Booker was put in charge of about 75 Indian youths unaccustomed to wearing new clothes or sitting in school all day. With the help of the black students, the Indians learned English and proved to be good students and workers.

When one the Indians had to return home because of illness, Booker was asked to escort him to Washington. On the way, he learned a few new lessons in *discrimination*. On a steamboat, the Indian was allowed into the dining room; Booker was not. A Washington hotel accommodated the Indian, but denied Booker a room.

At Hampton, the many young black men and women who could not pay their tuition in cash worked in the school's sawmills and laundries. General Armstrong opened a night school that they could attend after working all day. He put Booker in charge of this evening school.

At this time in history, some whites wanted to keep all blacks poor and dependent. Others saw the benefits of educating them, not only for the former slaves themselves, but for the national economy. The first all-black schools were sponsored and staffed by Northern whites, but some Southern states also began to see the need for black schools. In 1881, the state of Alabama allotted $2,000 to establish a school to train black teachers in the town of Tuskegee.

Aware of General Armstrong's work at Hampton, Alabama officials wrote to him, asking if he could recommend a white teacher from his staff to head their future school. General Armstrong replied that he could not think of a suitable white man, but if they would hire a black principal, he would send Booker T. Washington, the "best man we have ever had here."

About a week later, the Alabama officials agreed. Washington left Hampton for Tuskegee, beginning the mission that would become his life's work.

Washington led his first Tuskegee Institute students by example, chopping wood and getting his own hands dirty. Eventually, almost all of Tuskegee's 40 buildings would be erected by students like those shown here digging the foundation for the C. P. Huntington Memorial Building.

5

The Tuskegee Institute

When Booker T. Washington arrived in Alabama in June of 1881 to head the Tuskegee Institute, he discovered that there was no school. The state had allotted money for instructors' salaries, but none for land, buildings, or books. Washington did find one thing more valuable than money, though: whites living and working in harmony with the freed slaves who greatly outnumbered them. If and when Washington had a school to teach in, he felt that his work would be valued by blacks and whites alike. The politically active blacks in Tuskegee were starved for education and had petitioned the state to open the school. The two men who had written to Hampton and hired Washington were a former slave owner and a former slave.

Washington traveled about the county in a mule-drawn cart to learn about its people. The soil was rich, but the farmers grew no food, only cotton. They lived mostly on cornbread, fat pork, and black-eyed peas. They purchased clocks, sewing machines, and organs that they did not know how to use, and financed them on installment plans they could never pay off. All the while, their roofs leaked and they ate with their fingers out of skillets.

The school's first applicants were mostly teachers who knew little more than their students. The rest were younger blacks who wanted "book learning," which they thought would guarantee them easy jobs like teaching or preaching. But Washington knew how *futile* it would be for them to study Latin, Greek, or

French without learning practical skills with which to earn a living. The county depended on cotton crops, yet the students yearned for city life. Changing their *priorities* would be Booker's first challenge.

Before he could tackle the challenges of teaching, however, he needed a schoolhouse. He found a rickety old church with a shanty and got permission to use the structures. The makeshift school opened on July 4 with 30 men and women between the ages of 15 and 40. One month later, enrollment had grown to 50.

Washington needed help, and it soon arrived in the person of Miss Olivia Davidson, a light-skinned free black woman from Ohio. Trained as a teacher in Massachusetts, Miss Davidson taught classes and helped raise money for the school. She proved to be a tireless, effective fund-raiser, working among Northern whites as well as locals.

About three months after the school opened, an abandoned plantation came on the market. The big house had burned down, but a cabin, a stable, a kitchen, and a henhouse remained standing. The property, about a mile out of town, was offered for $500. Washington obtained a personal loan from the treasurer at Hampton and bought it.

The first classes were taught in the henhouse. After school hours each afternoon, Washington picked up an axe and led the students to work repairing the buildings and clearing the land for planting. At first, the would-be *intellectuals* and aspiring city dwellers in Washington's class were reluctant to do any manual labor. But when he showed them that even their principal did not consider himself above getting his hands dirty, they followed his example.

Enrollment at the Tuskegee Institute soon overran the small classrooms in the stable and the henhouse. Without new, larger buildings—and living quarters for the students—the school could not continue. Washington worked to earn

Female Tuskegee students making mattresses. At first, Tuskegee students made their own bricks, bedding, and furniture out of necessity. But they soon became skilled crafters who sold their handiwork to make money for the school and to pay their expenses.

the support of the entire community. White merchants provided building materials. Poor black farmers contributed a hog, a horse, or a half-dozen eggs—whatever they could give. Miss

Davidson traveled north to raise money, an activity that would always be critical to Tuskegee's survival. The students did the construction work, learning many valuable skills in the process. Eventually, the students would erect almost all of the 40 buildings at Tuskegee Institute.

A year after arriving in Tuskegee, Washington married Fannie Smith, his longtime sweetheart from Malden. Fannie had been one of Booker's pupils in Tinkersville and was also a Hampton graduate. The couple had a daughter, Portia, but Mrs. Washington died less than two years after their marriage. Booker was a widower at only 28 years of age. His grief did not slow down his efforts to improve his school, though.

Tuskegee students learned to make bricks, furniture, and carts. They grew most of their own food. These activities became sources of income for the school, as they produced more than they needed and sold the surplus. Washington was anxious to show his white neighbors that ex-slaves could become reliable tradesmen who contributed to the economy—if only they had the right education. At the same time, he was showing his black students that learning a trade could lead to a life of independence and prosperity. That, in turn, would earn them the respect, acceptance, and political equality they yearned for. Washington's belief in "slow progress" toward equal rights for blacks would eventually draw the criticism of some racial *activists*.

With money always in short supply, the first students at the growing campus endured many hardships. The cooks had no stove and no experience; the food was usually terrible. There were few dishes and no tables. Arguments over who got to use the kitchen's single coffee cup were commonplace.

Until the dormitories were built, the students slept in run-down cabins. They had no beds until they built them. They made mattresses by sewing large cloth bags and filling them with pine needles. They had no blankets during the first cold winter at the school. Despite these harsh conditions, Washington stressed personal cleanliness. He preached "the gospel of the toothbrush," a device most of the students had never seen before coming to Tuskegee.

Soon after he had arrived in Tuskegee, Washington sent for his brother John and made him the school's business agent. In 1885 Washington married Olivia Davidson. They had two children, Booker T., Jr., and Ernest. But his second wife, who had always been in delicate health, died four years after their marriage. In 1892 Washington married for the last time. His third wife, Maggie Murray, was a teacher and principal at Tuskegee. She brought her niece, Laura, to the marriage, and Booker had three children of his own. Maggie played a vital role in fund-raising and supervising the female students' industries, and she became active in national black women's organizations.

As its enrollment and faculty grew,

Tuskegee became known nationally. Wealthy *philanthropists* from the North made large contributions, often enough to pay for the construction of entire buildings. Washington was invited to speak at many gatherings in both the North and the South. Despite strict *segregation* throughout the South, Washington was often able to cross racial barriers. He was not always comfortable sitting with white friends and *benefactors* on trains or in dining rooms in the South, but once his identity was known, he usually faced no discrimination.

In 1895, Washington became the first black ever to share a public speaking platform with white politicians at the Cotton States and International Exposition in Atlanta, Georgia. He won his white audience over by outlining his *philosophy* of education and self-improvement as the keys to black progress, rather than pushing for immediate equality. "It is important that all privileges of the law be ours," he said, "but it is vastly more important that we be prepared for

the exercises of these privileges." Washington's speech became known as the Atlanta Compromise speech.

For all of Tuskegee's successes, its founder still thought something was missing: an *agriculture* department. Washington never forgot the

Washington hired George Washington Carver (shown here) to head Tuskegee's agriculture department. During his 49-year career at Tuskegee, Carver not only became a world-famous botanist, but also taught black sharecroppers how to farm more productively.

poverty he had seen among the black *sharecroppers* who lived around the school. They had worn out the soil growing nothing but cotton for many years, unaware of the benefits of crop rotation. They also lacked the knowledge to successfully grow vegetables. It took Washington

15 years to gather the resources to begin an agriculture department. He hired George Washington Carver to lead it. Carver gained a worldwide reputation as a naturalist and *botanist* during his nearly 50 years at Tuskegee.

Washington had high expectations for all of his Tuskegee instructors: he hired Carver to be a teacher, experimenter, veterinarian, and crop producer—and to landscape the campus in his spare time. Carver did not disappoint him. Together they developed the Tuskegee Negro Conference, which brought black sharecroppers to the school to learn how to grow new crops and to take better care of the ones they already grew. Carver wrote simple pamphlets that were distributed to farmers all over the South. He also bred hardier seeds and developed new methods of farming.

Washington also organized *seminars* for blacks who wanted to learn how to start up small businesses. These seminars grew into the Negro Business League, with 300 branches across the country. He used all of these forums to preach his philosophy of accommodation in dealing with whites. Washington favored avoiding politics and was against agitating for change. He urged maintaining personal dignity and striving for economic independence.

"Don't push" was his motto.

But as the 19th century ended, other black organizations whose motto was "Push" were gaining strength.

By 1915, *when this photo was taken, Washington had devoted 35 years of his life to the Tuskegee Institute, transforming it from an abandoned plantation into a world-renowned school.*

6

Completing a Mission

By 1898, after 17 years of building and running the Tuskegee Institute, Washington had gained international prestige as a leader of his people and as an educator. He had lunched with President William McKinley, for instance, during a rally in Chicago celebrating the end of the Spanish-American War. His nonstop workload exhausted him. In the spring of 1899, he took a much-needed three-month vacation in Europe. There he met many dignitaries, including the reigning British monarch, Queen Victoria, with whom he had tea at Windsor Castle.

But race relations in America were not as peaceful as they were in Booker T. Washington's social circle. The Ku Klux Klan was gaining strength; black men were being lynched by white men at a terrifying rate. The Klansmen responsible for these acts of violence went unpunished. Washington's refusal to become more *militant* turned some black leaders against him. The division between Washington and those who accused him of turning a blind eye to racial injustice in order to keep his powerful white friends happy never healed.

In 1901 Washington published *Up from Slavery*, his *autobiography*. The story of his rise from poverty to prominence drew a favorable response for its inspiring message. It was translated into many languages and helped bring an influx of donations to the Tuskegee Institute from wealthy businessmen and industrialists.

That same year President Theodore Roosevelt invited him to dine at the White

President Theodore Roosevelt, standing between Booker T. and Margaret Murray Washington, is honored during a visit to the Tuskegee Institute. Washington's association with President Roosevelt angered white supremacists and black activists alike.

House, provoking an uproar in the newspapers. Washington was attacked for mingling with whites even though in his speeches he suggested that the races should remain separate in social matters. Roosevelt was attacked for consulting a black man on the nation's business. The president personally saw nothing wrong with what he did, but he never invited another black guest to the White House.

Washington continued to communicate with the president, urging him to appoint blacks to federal positions. Despite loud opposition from white supremacists (people who believe whites are better than blacks and should enjoy a privileged place in society), Roosevelt did accept some of Washington's recommendations. Relying on his good reputation among whites, Washington sought to extend his political influence by bringing together a group of successful black politicians, businessmen, and educators who supported his philosophy. His prestige made him the most prominent spokesman for his race. It also made him enemies among rival black leaders who had different ideas.

Strong and outspoken white groups tried to smother black political and civil rights. Some

Southern states passed laws that made it almost impossible for blacks to vote. The more politically active Washington became, the more enemies he made. His belief that poor, uneducated blacks were no more qualified to vote than poor, uneducated whites was seen as a sellout by some blacks. Some of his speaking appearances ended in fights and riots incited by his black opponents. Black newspapers charged that Washington's approach had led to a decline in the progress of their people since the revolutionary days following the emancipation (freeing) of slaves.

A rival leader, W. E. B. Du Bois, emerged and a public struggle for power erupted. Although Du Bois had praised Washington's Atlanta Compromise speech of 1895, he felt that the time for meekly tiptoeing toward racial equality had passed. Du Bois favored demanding immediate civil rights and full equality for blacks. He denounced Washington's more moderate methods as timid and ineffective.

Black leader W. E. B. Du Bois (shown here) demanded immediate racial equality and urged blacks to attend colleges rather than trade schools. He strongly disagreed with Washington's belief that blacks needed to learn trades and contribute to the economy before they could expect equal rights.

Washington arranged a three-day conference in New York to heal their rift, but the meeting ended with both sides as far apart as ever.

Du Bois believed that the top 10 percent

of black scholars—a group he called "the Talented Tenth"—should go to college instead of, or in addition to, receiving training at Tuskegee. He also thought the government or charities should pay for those who could not afford it. Washington had nothing against blacks going to college—his daughter, Portia, entered Wellesley College for women in 1901—but he was more concerned about the other 90 percent of blacks, who would need to learn skilled trades if they wanted to improve their lives. Washington also believed that those who worked their way through school became stronger than those who were "coddled" with free educations.

Du Bois tried to organize a black group to seize leadership of the race from Washington, but his efforts failed. Washington was backed by such prominent whites as the wealthy industrialist Andrew Carnegie, who was among many distinguished guests in attendance at Tuskegee's 25th anniversary celebration in 1906.

Wherever Washington traveled to speak, he was greeted enthusiastically. In the days before radio or television, the only way people could see and hear the famous *orators* and statesmen was in person. Washington seldom left a city or town without generous donations from its leading citizens. White multimillionaires like John D. Rockefeller and Andrew Carnegie were among Tuskegee's regular contributors. Former and future presidents visited the school or attended fund-raisers in the North. Washington remained the country's most visible black leader and the black man most respected by influential whites.

But his constant bickering with his black opponents and his ceaseless work and travel took their toll. In 1903 he took another vacation to Europe, but he kept himself informed at all times on every detail of what was happening at his school.

Washington remained convinced that industrial training was more valuable than aca-

demics for young blacks. His decision to empha-
size such skills as blacksmithing and wheel-
wrighting at the expense of book learning upset
his academic faculty. They were also uncomfort-
able with Washington's *scrutiny* of their activities, both in and out of the classroom. He
controlled every aspect of the school, and he was
not easily satisfied. He set high standards—and
quickly fired anyone who failed to meet them.
The Tuskegee Institute had become his whole
life.

Washington's efforts had paid off.
Tuskegee was now known all over the world.
Visitors from as far away as China and Japan
came to the rural Alabama campus to observe
and to learn.

Three events during Washington's later
years would leave him feeling deeply disap-
pointed by his high-ranking white friends. In
1906, a shooting in the small town of
Brownsville, Texas, left one white man dead
and a policeman wounded. Local citizens

blamed black soldiers stationed at a nearby army base. Ignoring Washington's plea for further investigation, President Roosevelt ordered the dishonorable discharge of 167 of the soldiers. A month later, a mob of white men in Atlanta attacked the city's black community and ran wild for five days, destroying property and killing 10 blacks. The president did nothing to put down the riot.

In 1908, a race riot in Springfield, Illinois, made national headlines, drowning out Washington's message of moderation. The more radical and militant black leaders joined with outraged whites in calling for a conference of both races to seek solutions to the problems of prejudice and inequality. Washington was invited, but when he learned that several of his black enemies would be there, he decided to stay away. Out of that conference and another held a year later emerged the National Association for the Advancement of Colored People (NAACP). Washington never became associated with the

When he realized he was dying, Washington demanded release from a New York City hospital, saying, "I was born in the South, I have lived and labored in the South, and I expect to die and be buried in the South." His last wish was granted on November 16, 1915, when his body was buried on the Tuskegee campus.

organization. His failure to address many instances of racial discrimination had deafened many people to his voice. But the Tuskegee Institute's reputation never diminished, and its mission never changed. Washington's last endeavor at the school that had been his life's work was starting an annual health conference to foster the well-being of black people.

During his last years, Washington became more outspoken against segregation of the races, inadequate schools for blacks, the obstruction of black voting rights, and the unchecked violence of the Klan and lynch mobs. While his black opponents welcomed his protests, they also believed them to be too little, too late.

During a speaking tour in New York City in November of 1915, he became ill. Feeling his life ebbing away, Washington boarded a train for home on November 12. He died about eight hours after arriving in Tuskegee at the age of 59.

Even his severest critic, W. E. B. Du Bois, said of him, "He was the greatest Negro leader since Frederick Douglass."

The Tuskegee Institute remains a center of learning today, a monument to his mission: to improve the physical, moral, and economic standing of African-American people. Booker T. Washington's name still brings to mind leadership and academic excellence—and the ongoing pursuit of equality for everyone.

Further Reading

Nicholson, Lois P. *George Washington Carver*. New York: Chelsea House Publishers, 1994.

Patterson, Lillie. *Booker T. Washington: Leader of His People*. Illustrated by Anthony D'Adamo. New York: Chelsea House Publishers, 1991.

Schroeder, Alan. *Booker T. Washington*. New York: Chelsea House Publishers, 1992.

Stafford, Mark. *W. E. B. Du Bois*. New York: Chelsea House Publishers, 1989.

Washington, Booker T. *My Larger Education*. Garden City, N.Y.: Doubleday, 1911.

———. *Up from Slavery*. 1901. Reprint. New York: Viking Penguin, 1986.

Chronology

1856	Booker T. Washington is born in Hale's Ford, Virginia, on or around April 5
1865	Booker moves with his mother and siblings to join his stepfather in Malden, West Virginia
1872	After years of working and attending the black school in nearby Tinkersville, Booker journeys to Hampton, Virginia, to study at the Hampton Normal and Agricultural Institute
1875	After graduating from Hampton, Booker T. Washington returns to Malden and teaches at the Tinkersville school
1879	Washington gets a job teaching at Hampton

1881	He opens the Tuskegee Institute in Tuskegee, Alabama
1882	Washington marries Fannie Smith
1883	The Washingtons' daughter, Portia, is born
1884	Fannie Washington dies
1885	Booker T. Washington marries his second wife, Olivia Davidson; their son, Booker T., Jr., is born
1889	Another son, Ernest Davidson, is born; Olivia Washington dies
1892	Booker T. Washington marries his third wife, Margaret Murray
1895	He delivers his famous Atlanta Compromise speech at the Cotton States and International Exposition in Atlanta, Georgia, on September 18

1901   *Up from Slavery* is published; Washington dines in the White House on October 16

1904   Booker T. Washington adopts his wife's niece, Laura Murray

1915   He dies on November 13 in Tuskegee; buried November 16 on the grounds of the institute

Glossary

activists	people who believe in taking action such as a march or a protest to make their opinion known on an issue
agriculture	the science of growing crops and raising livestock
arduous	hard or strenuous
autobiography	a person's life story written in his or her own words
benefactors	people who provide financial support
botanist	a scientist who studies plant life
carpetbaggers	Northerners who traveled to the South after the Civil War, often to take advantage of newly freed slaves
commencement	a ceremony in which people graduate from school
curriculum	the classes offered by a particular school
discrimination	unfair treatment on the basis of race
dormitory	living and sleeping quarters for students

economic	related to the pattern of making, buying, and selling goods in a particular place
futile	serving no real purpose
inadequate	not good enough or too small in quantity
intellectuals	people with great or highly developed mental ability
liberal arts	studies intended to increase a person's general knowledge rather than to teach him or her a specific profession
lynching	the hanging of someone by people who take the law into their own hands
militant	extremely active in support of a cause
orators	talented or well-trained public speakers
persuasively	in a moving or convincing manner
philanthropists	people who donate money to schools, hospitals, or charities that promote the welfare of others
philosophy	the basic beliefs that guide a person or group
plantation	a large farm, especially one worked by slave labor in the South before the Civil War

priorities tasks, problems, or duties that need a person's attention

scrutiny very close study of someone or something

segregation separation of blacks and whites, formerly enforced by law in the United States

seminars meetings to share and discuss information

sharecroppers farmers, especially in the South, who live as tenants; they pay their landlords with a percentage of their crops

staples items such as flour and sugar that are produced in large amounts and used by many people

Index

Lois P. Nicholson is a native of Sudlersville, Maryland. She holds a bachelor of science degree in elementary education and a master's degree in education from the Salisbury State University. She is a school library media specialist at Elkridge Elementary near Baltimore. In addition to *Booker T. Washington*, she has written the following biographies for young readers: *George Washington Carver: Botanist and Ecologist, Oprah Winfrey: Entertainer, Helen Keller, Michael Jackson, Casey Stengel, Nolan Ryan, Oprah Winfrey* (Chelsea House); *Cal Ripken, Jr.: Quiet Hero* (Tidewater); *Georgia O'Keeffe* (Lucent); and *Babe Ruth: Sultan of Swat* (Goodwood Press). In addition to writing, Nicholson visits schools and speaks to students and faculties about writing nonfiction. She is the mother of two grown children and lives in Baltimore.

Picture Credits

Every effort has been made to contact the copyright owners of photographs and illustrations used in this book. In the event that the holder of a copyright has not heard from us, he or she should contact Chelsea House Publishers.

2: Special Collections, New York Public Library
6: Library of Congress, #62-5334
10: National Park Service, Booker T. Washington National Monument
11: National Park Service, Booker T. Washington National Monument
14: National Park Service, Booker T. Washington National Monument
21: Courtesy of Virginia State Library & Archives

26: Archives & Manuscripts Division, West Virginia University Library
33: Courtesy of Tuskegee University Archives
38: Courtesy of Tuskegee University Archives
43: Archives & Manuscripts Collection, Hampton University, Hampton, Virginia
46: Archives & Manuscripts Collection, Hampton University, Hampton, Virginia

50: Library of Congress, #J694-99
55: Library of Congress, #J694-13
60-61: Tuskegee Institute/Walter Scott, Photographer
64: Courtesy of Tuskegee University Archives
67: Courtesy of Tuskegee University Archives
70: Schomburg Center For Research In Black Culture, NYPL
75: Courtesy of Tuskegee University Archives